SURFACE-FEEDING SEA FISH

JOHN BICKERDYKE

WE have now fished many waters in many ways ; journeyed round the coasts of Great Britain—fly fishing here, pater-nostering there, casting out our spinning or other tackle from land or pierhead ; now and again, when the sea was not too lumpy, trusting ourselves in small craft ; and, going further afield in yachts or large fishing boats, have sought such sport as the deeper water affords. We have even set lobster, crab, and prawn pots, and hunted among the rocks with iron hooks for fierce congers. During that voyage home from India there was ocean fishing in tropical seas for the giant fish of the mackerel species ; and, in addition, we carefully examined into the several advantages of various baits which may or may not be obtainable, as the case may be. With such experience we should have acquired a good general knowledge of sea fishing ; but there still remains much to be learnt concerning the habits, peculiarities, and certain not-hitherto-noticed special means of capturing, the more sporting sea fish.

First, for they deserve the place of honour, come those fish which commonly or frequently swim or feed near the surface, and are to be caught with fly or whiffing tackle. The most important of these undoubtedly is—

The BASS, the *labrax* of Aristotle, and *lupus* of Pliny. This most admirable fish is nothing more nor less than a large marine perch which, when it enters estuaries for spawning pur-poses at the end of summer, sometimes proceeds up rivers into fresh water. Indeed, it is said that the Romans not only kept bass in captivity, but also bred them in aquaria filled with spring water. Mr. Arnold, of Guernsey, repeated this experiment—omitting the breeding part of it—not only with success, but went so far as to say that the flesh of the fish was greatly improved by the sojourn in fresh water.

Though anglers who have cast their lines among shoals of these fish and caught nothing, may question the fact, there is not much doubt that the sea perch were anciently called wolves on account of their voracity, and, perhaps, also because of a certain sense of cunning they appear to possess when surrounding the sand-eels, young herrings, and mackerel, &c., on which they largely feed. They have various local names : in Kentish waters are often termed *sea dace*, while at Herne Bay they are dignified by the name of *white salmon*. In Scotland, where they are very scarce, they are sometimes termed *gape mouths* ; while at Belfast the people persistently call them *white mullet*, or *king of the mullets*.

In form the bass is less graceful than the dace of fresh water, but is built on finer lines than the chub, and may be always recognised by the prickly dorsal fin, similar to that worn by the freshwater perch. The back is dark blue, while the sides and belly are silvery. It has a liberal allowance of teeth, some placed in crescent shape on the roof of its mouth, others in a small patch at the base of the tongue. Its mouth otherwise is very leathery and tough, and, so far, very different from that of the mullet. With regard to size, a ten or twelve pounder must be considered a large fish, though occasionally one of 15 lbs. is caught by the angler. Yarrell mentions one of 28 lbs., but I must confess to being somewhat distrustful of the weights of fish given by the older ichthyologists. It is said that a bass of 22 lbs. was once netted near Herne Bay Pier. A friend tells me he had an account of a bass weighing 24½ lbs. after being cleaned, from a trustworthy man who himself caught the fish.

For angling purposes bass may be divided into two classes : those which run from about two pounds to five pounds, and may sometimes be seen in immense shoals, hunting sand-eels or fry ;

and the large and more aged fish which, in the dusk of early morning, will be seen swimming in stately fashion in little companies of two to five in number, or thereabouts, close to the edge of steep rocks, round wooden piers and jetties, and among the old woodwork of harbours. It is these large, shy, old fish which the enthusiastic bass fisher feels it an honour and a duty to catch. They are the Thames trout of the sea. But for lively and continued ·sport commend me rather to the shoals of smaller bass when well on the feed. On many days even these cannot be caught, though to all appearance they are savagely and hungrily chasing their unfortunate prey. As in freshwater fishing, much depends upon the weather. If it be very bright and sunny the fish are scared by the line, and are not to be deceived into deeming a piece of indiarubber band a succulent worm or a baby eel. Under such conditions baits to be tried are the curb-chain spinner (p. 130) or a white unvarnished sole-skin phantom with silvered head. The angler, however, will catch nothing unless he keeps out of sight and the boat is worked noiselessly.

From an English bass-fisher's point of view, the most interesting parts of our coast are those bordering Devonshire and Cornwall, portions of Wales, and the Island of Anglesea. Sometimes they are fairly plentiful in or near the estuary of the Thames, as, for instance, at Herne Bay. Not that bass are wanting elsewhere, for they can occasionally be found, even in considerable numbers, on the East coast, as far north as Scotland, and even Norway, where, however, bass are very scarce. In Ireland they are caught on the east and south coasts, and I have known large shoals enter the Shannon estuary, and swim up the mouth of a tributary river. Probably, when sea fishing is still further recognised as a sport, places will be found on the Irish coast where bass are very plentiful.

Speaking generally, the bass is a summer fish, not leaving the deep sea and approaching the coast until the mild weather sets in. Much depends on the state of the weather. If it be cold their coming will be delayed, while in warm, genial seasons they may be expected somewhat earlier than usual. On the coast of Devonshire bass have been captured as early as February, but it is usually March or April before any quantity is observed. Thence onwards, until the cold weather comes again and drives them into deep water, these fish will be found, either in shoals or singly, off headlands, in races, playing about the bars of rivers, and towards the end of the summer entering the estuaries in large numbers. Sometimes they are feeding on the surface, sometimes on the bottom. While the youngsters play about in the sharp running water and perpetrate fierce onslaughts on shoals of innocent sand-eels and herring fry, the more elderly fish, as I have pointed out, coast round the rocks, and enter harbours and other places where there is plenty of refuse for them to feed upon. In such situations their tastes appear to degenerate, for they will often scornfully turn away from a delicate sand-eel presented to them alive, while a malodorous piece of oily ray's liver they will suck in greedily.

There are few baits bass will not take at times ; but, as I have pointed out, where fish develop a taste for scavengering, their tastes must be pampered, and if ray's liver is not available the entrails of chicken or rabbit (if somewhat high so much the better) may often be used with success. Of squid, cuttle and octopus they are particularly fond. The largest bass I ever hooked came like a tiger at a piece of squid I was using as a bait for conger, one night off the Welsh coast. I was handlining, and thinking I had an eel on, which would have to be hauled by main force away from the rocks, I brought this fish up to the surface in double quick time. There he rolled and splashed in a bath of incandescent silver as it were, for the water which he lashed with his tail was full of phosphorescence. He brought such consternation to the heart of the little Welsh lad who was with me, that the youth of many consonants to his unpronounceable name was too unnerved to use the gaff, and while I was abjuring him to do his duty the hook came away, the great fish disappeared, and nothing was left but flecks of phosphorescence on the surface of the dark water. He was every ounce of fifteen pounds. Indeed I might add another five pounds to his weight, and who can contradict me? There is the one redeeming point about a lost fish. It is the proud privilege of the lamenting angler to fix the weight of the dear departed without the least fear of contradiction.

But to return to the bait question. Among the shoals which are feeding in some tidal race during the best of the flood tide, the bait should certainly be somewhat similar to the fry on which they are feeding. A strip of fish skin, the Sarcelle bait, a sand-eel, or a very small mackerel, all these may be tried.

Sometimes the fly fisher meets with great success. Among the many flies which may be used, I doubt if any are better than the Whitebait fly (see p. 135), the Shaldon Shiner, and the Goldfinch. The dressing of the Shaldon Shiner has already been given (p. 149). The Goldfinch is a well-known salmon fly, which is dressed as follows : Tag, gold tinsel and black floss ; tail, a golden pheasant topping ; body, gold-coloured floss ; pale yellow hackle ; blue jay at shoulder ; gold tinsel ; wing composed entirely of toppings ; red macaw ribs and black head. But bass fishers generally tell you that a piece of fish skin—gurnet belly for preference—cast like a fly is more killing than feathers and tinsel.

Above all things, the boat must not be taken right through or even very near the shoal. If the angler has not the skill or necessary tackle to cast among the fish, the boat should be worked across the tide in the fashion known as harling, a method very carefully described on pages 240 and 241. From a moored boat drift lines or float tackle is used, the tide carrying the bait down to the fish. If a small *live* fish of any kind, such as smelt, sand-eel, or flat fish, can be obtained for bait, so much the better. The current will often work a spinning bait.

It is not always necessary to moor the boat when drift-line fishing, for the crew can continue pulling steadily, and so keep the little craft in about the right position. In that case it is a good plan when a fish is hooked to edge the boat well to one side of the shoal, drop down with the tide while reeling in, and play him below the uncaught bass. If the water is at all clear this plan, which the fly fisher should also bear in mind, will prevent disturbing the fish and lead to further captures. If it is thick and the fish are taking freely, it may in some cases amount to a loss of time with no corresponding benefit, but it is very seldom that the manœuvre does not repay the trouble involved.

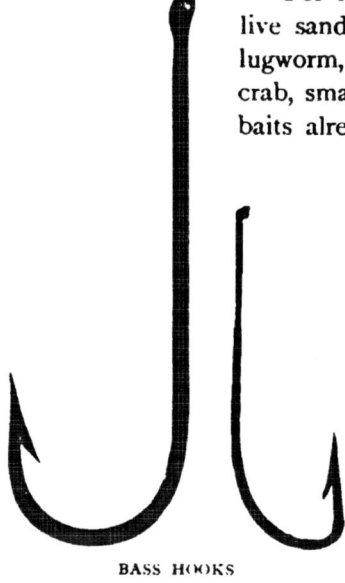

For fishing from rocks or piers the live sand-eel may be tried, or ray's liver, lugworm, squid, a piece of mackerel, soft crab, small flat fish, or other of the many baits already mentioned. Where the fish can be approached, some ray's liver should be placed in a coarse sack and fastened to a cord and sunk by means of stones. The perfumed oils emanating from this scent-packet are very likely to attract the fish to the spot, where, if they find a tenderly arranged morsel of ray's liver awaiting them, they will surely appreciate the thoughtfulness of the angler and meet his wishes in the matter.

BASS HOOKS

For use on the bottom with a leger, as, for instance, on the sandy shore of an estuary, there are few baits better than a strip of squid, but ray's liver is equally killing in some places. For these and some other baits the large round bend hook shown in the illustration is suitable. If the fish run small, or the bait is insignificant, use two or three sizes smaller. It may be either round bend or the Pennell-Limerick illustrated. A round bend gets a better hold round bones and cartilages than a narrow hook of abrupt angle.

A capital plan—one followed a good deal at Brixham, both in the harbour and outside—is to thread a small fish on a No. 3 or 4 Exeter round bend hook. This is done by means of a baiting needle which brings the snooding in at the mouth of the bait and out at its tail ; in fact, the arrangement closely resembles the gorge trolling bait of pike fishers. The snooding need not be very long. To it is attached a somewhat fine unleaded line. The bait is thrown overboard and allowed to lie on the bottom. When a bass takes it he must feel no resistance whatever, and should be given a few seconds to swallow it and go off with four or five yards of line. Those who read Mr. Harmsworth's contribution will no doubt notice the resemblance between this method and tarpon fishing. In the harbour the favourite bait is a piece of squid or liver, the same unleaded tackle being used. These harbour fish are so excessively wide awake that if they feel the pull from a lead they at once drop the bait. A rod can, and in most cases should, be used with this tackle. A bait I see I have not mentioned is the guts of the pilchard, which all fish love. They make a most excellent ground bait, particularly if mixed up with pounded crabs.

In considering what tackle and baits to use, the angler must look at all the conditions of depth, colour of the water, nature of bottom, distance from the fish, &c., and endeavour to decide which of the various methods of angling mentioned will best enable him to put the right bait in front of the fish. There is really no royal road to fishing, and rule-of-thumb work will more often than not simply lead to failure. In the case of bass, and still more of mullet, the angler has to pit his brains against some of the most cautious and cunning of the fish which swim in the sea. Indeed, of large mullet it may be said that, though perhaps not more wary than big bass, they are infinitely more difficult to capture than the highly educated chalk-stream trout or the venerable carp of some ancient fish stew.

Tiros must not expect to catch many big bass in a day. If

they land an eight-pounder they may well regard it as a triumph. For numbers they must seek the whereabouts of the school bass, and if fortune favours them, and they and their boatmen are fairly expert, they may weigh their fish by the hundred-weight at the end of the day. That veteran amateur sea fisherman, Mr. J. C. Wilcocks, by whose teaching in his admirable work on sea fishing I and many more greatly profited in years gone by, has told how once, fishing with a friend close to Berry Point, at Teignmouth, five hundredweight of bass were caught. I doubt if there is anyone else living who has met with such extraordinary success ; indeed, if everyone were to kill bass in this wholesale way, in the next edition of this work the article on 'Labrax lupus' might be omitted.

The GREY MULLET, like the bass, has a prickly dorsal fin. It is very easily distinguished from its more voracious companion by the fact that this fin contains only four very evident spines, while that of the bass contains eight. The mouth of the mullet, too, is small and only suited for soft food. Of these fish there are two kinds, the great grey mullet (*Mugil capito*) and the lesser grey mullet (*Mugil chelo*), the latter being very abundant in some South-coast harbours, and sometimes as easy of capture as the great grey mullet is difficult. A distinction between the two varieties is the number of rays in the tail fin, the larger kind, which is also called the 'thin-lipped mullet,' having seventeen, while the lesser, or thick-lipped mullet, has fifteen.

Of red, or surmullet, beloved of the Romans, I need say nothing, for these fish are very rarely captured, except in nets, either by the sportsman or the professional fisherman, only now and again succumbing to the charms of a harbour-bred rag-worm, more particularly in the neighbourhood of very foul drains. I commend this point to the attention of those who deem red mullet worthless unless served *à la* woodcock. A good many are caught in trammel nets.

Grey mullet are gregarious and very plentiful in some estuaries and harbours, Chichester, Littlehampton, Plymouth,

GREY MULLET—'FOLLOWING UP THE TIDE'.

Weymouth, and the mouth of the Stour being favourite haunts of theirs. They appear to be as much at home in fresh water as in salt. At one time shoals were to be found in Oulton Broad, entering there, no doubt, when the lock was open, or, perhaps, making their way by the Yare and journeying round to Mutford.

In the thirties a gentleman named Arnold, living at Guernsey, sent a communication to the Zoological Society of London, concerning some interesting observations he had made on mullet kept in a five-acre lake which for nine months in the year was filled with fresh water. In summer the sea entered the lake through a tunnel. There were several varieties of sea fish in the enclosure, including a large number of mullet which appeared to breed freely. I have no doubt that mullet could be introduced with advantage into many a semi-tidal pool, provided there were a sufficient depth of water.

A very curious experiment was recorded in connection with the placing of a mullet which had been accustomed to the Baltic (where the amount of saline matter is small) in North Sea water in which there was three times as much salt. The fish was forced to float. For about three hours it made ineffectual attempts to keep below the surface, and then died. From observations made in an aquarium, it seems that mullet are in the habit of sucking sand into their mouths, almost immediately afterwards sending out the coarser particles. By a beautifully arranged natural filter, hard substances of any considerable size cannot find their way into the stomach, nor can sand get access to the gills ; for this reason, therefore, it is absolutely necessary that any bait used for mullet should be soft, and the hook should be small. If the hook were too large, it would be rejected and the bait retained.

Following up the tide into estuaries and harbours, these shy fish feed greedily, sucking in various odds and ends of partly decomposed matter, silkweed, ragworms, fish garbage, and the like. They will swim after a ship that has come from abroad into dock, and work all over its bottom with their snouts, eating the softer seaweeds and small marine insects.

Mullet are very easily tamed, and, being susceptible to sound, have been known to assemble for dinner on hearing the knocking noise of the chopper employed to prepare their food. So acute is the hearing of these creatures, that old mullet fishers would never dream of shouting to one another, and when rowing after a shoal, the men, if careful, will muffle their oars.

The thick-lipped variety is much more widely distributed than are the large grey mullet. Quantities have been seen in Belfast Lough and other parts of Ireland. From June to September they are found on the coasts of the Orkneys and Zetland, and also on the eastern and western shores of Scotland. Of all the sporting fish of the sea, grey mullet are the most difficult to capture and among the gamest when hooked. There are times when the lesser variety will feed ravenously, and are caught in large numbers on a paternoster baited with a live ragworm ; but the big fellows that we see with their broad dark backs swimming round the piles in harbours, or under the old-fashioned wooden jetties and piers, are singularly cautious so far as taking a baited hook into their mouths is concerned. In the matter of showing themselves their timidity is not apparent. Sometimes they are speared or harpooned, and there is a legend of an Italian gentleman who caught many fish in this way from Margate Jetty.

These fish are as difficult to net as they are to secure with hook and line. When first surrounded there is, to use the words of the reporter, 'a scene of great confusion' ; but presently they become organised, and elect a leader who carefully examines the net for holes, and, failing to find any, leaps over the buoy rope, the rest following. In the Mediterranean the fishermen sometimes heighten their net above the surface by means of pieces of cane. Another plan is to sprinkle a little straw or sawdust on the water inside the net. The mullet then seem unable to distinguish between the rope and the straw, and take short leaps. At Naples the fishermen sometimes place rafts made of reeds close to the outside of the nets encircling the mullet, so that when the fish leap they fall on to the rafts and are captured. In English waters a trammel net is often found deadly.

Sometimes enormous takes of grey mullet are made in seines. One of the biggest hauls on record occurred in January of this year (1895). A quantity of these fish was seen in Whitesand Bay, Land's End. The Sennen Cove fishermen were sent for and shot their nets by moonlight, about ten o'clock at night. About twelve thousand mullet, averaging something like 4 lbs. each, were surrounded. Many of them weighed as much as 8 lbs. This was a very unusual and very valuable catch, the fish, which weighed several tons, selling for 600*l.* The take seemed so remarkable, that I doubted the accuracy of the figures and wrote to the postmaster of St. Just on the subject. He kindly assures me that the report is perfectly correct, and adds that the buyers who sent the fish to Paris made a very bad bargain.

Angling for these shy fish is like an incurable disease —there are many prescriptions for it. Some of these, I fear, do not stand the test of time and are merely based on chance successes, depending more on the humour of the fish than the attractiveness of the bait or 'cute arrangement of tackle. The great point in mullet fishing is to use ground bait, not, as I have previously explained, so much for the purpose of attracting fish as of lulling their suspicions. Those who have studied the chapter on Baits may remember that some years ago I suggested to the director of the Marine Biological Association that macaroni might be used as a vehicle for the bait extracts which a chemist employed by the Association was preparing. Whether experiments were ever tried with the substance, I cannot say. But now, behold ! while I am at work on this chapter a sea fisherman, Mr. John Kirby, under the pseudonym of J. A. C. K., sends a most entertaining and practical account of mullet fishing to the ' Field,' in which he appears to prove most conclusively that the one really successful bait for large grey mullet is macaroni.

This gives me some hope that the Italian paste, either flavoured or not with some biological preparation, will prove a useful substitute for the mussels, pilchards, and other natural baits which the professional fishermen have so much difficulty in obtaining.

J. A. C. K. catches his mullet in this wise. His fishing ground is in the Fleet, a great backwater which separates the Chesil beach, west of Portland Roads, from the mainland of Dorsetshire and lies midway between Weymouth and Portland. Two bridges cross it, one carrying the railway, and the other—known as the Passage Bridge—the public carriage road. At times this water teems with mullet, and occasionally big bass put in an appearance. The best mullet fishing is done during the ease of the tide. J. A. C. K.'s tackle consists of a stiff eighteen-foot greenheart salmon rod, a large Nottingham reel carrying 200 yards of hemp line, ten feet of stout salmon gut, at the end of which is a Pennell-Limerick No. 8 hook. Above it are five or six other hook links of medium salmon gut, six or seven inches long, lapped to the main length on gut at

HOOK FOR MULLET WITH MACARONI BAIT

intervals of eighteen inches or thereabouts. Two feet above the bottom hook is a pistol bullet which is split and squeezed on to three inches of fine copper wire, the ends of the wire being lapped round the gut at a knot. The hook baits are pieces of ordinary macaroni pudding, and the gathering or ground bait boiled macaroni chopped up fine. Each bait consists of about three-quarters of an inch of macaroni which is big enough in the tube to admit the hook without splitting. The hooks have to be carefully covered and hidden. When everything is ready the angler takes the running line above the point where the gut is joined to it and presses it into the slit of a wine cork which acts as a float.

The next proceeding is to lay the rod against the parapet and, after pulling a sufficient quantity of line off the reel, to throw the bait into the water, and then lower the baited hooks (for the moment using the tackle as a hand line) under and against the very noses of the fish. The bright-looking baits, so says J. A. C. K., soon attract a goodly congregation of fish, which inspect them, smell them, touch them with their sensitive lips, deliberate upon them, and apparently come to the decision that they are most excellent food for mullet, but dangerous. Therefore they absolutely decline to partake of the feast in the form set before them. Presently a big old fellow will whisk smartly round and deliver a stroke with his tail which knocks off the bait ; a friend below opens his wide lips and the bait disappears. The other baits are knocked off in the same contemptuous way and eaten. The angler smiles, says nothing, and rebaits his hooks. Next he throws in some ground bait, and I confess I do not see why this proceeding should not have taken place earlier. This gathering or anti-suspicion bait is common macaroni boiled with skimmed milk and sugar and chopped up into quarter-inch lengths. As it sinks, the mullet, which as likely as not are feeding on the bottom, rise up, perhaps showing themselves, and take it greedily. While they are busily feeding flop go the baited hooks again into the very middle of them. Almost immediately a big fish will, or may, take in one of the baits ; but it is a long affair, this getting food into the mouth of a mullet, and the time to strike is not yet. In a few seconds the float sinks, a decided backward twitch is given to the line, and the fish is hooked.

All this time the rod has been leaning against the parapet of the bridge, quietly and harmlessly. Many a shy fish has been put down by seeing a long wooden wand waving about between it and the bright sky. J. A. C. K.'s plan after hooking a fish is to give him the butt remorselessly, in fact treat him as one would a salmon which was being played, or rather held, a few yards above a considerable waterfall.

The mullet has a tender mouth, and it might be supposed that harsh proceedings of this kind were fatal to success, but some mullet anglers declare that there is less likelihood of the hook cutting out when the fish is played roughly from the very onset than if he were dealt gently with and kept on the hook a considerable time ; perhaps this is very much a matter of opinion. Certainly strong measures adopted from the very beginning of the battle sometimes appear to cow fish and take all the nerve and pluck out of them. The method described is suitable for fishing when the tide is slack. At the beginning of the flood or ebb, four or five split wine corks should be added at even distances to buoy the tackle. Throw in an extra allowance of ground bait, and drop the baited hooks just over it, so that all float away together.

One opinion I will venture ; that now J. A. C. K. has let out the secret of his success (by the way, he catches bass as well as mullet in this manner), a troop of sea fishers will forthwith journey to the bridge over the Fleet and give those unfortunate mullet such a dose of the bait that it will be a case of *toujours macaroni*, and some other lure will have to be invented. It must not be supposed, however, that J. A. C. K. or anyone else has been invariably successful with large grey mullet. It took this ingenious fisherman six or seven weeks to bag his first mullet. If he caught one he was content, if two he was pleased. Two mullet averaging 8 lbs. each and a bass of 14 lbs. was the biggest bag. These were taken in about an hour at the top of the flood, and were the outcome of about ten fish run. Blank days were frequent, and would be expected in a neck-of-a-bottle tideway, slack water in which the gathering bait could abide round the hook baits being the essential condition precedent to the mullet taking to the hook freely. One hour's suitable water was the most that could be reckoned on daily. With regard to J. A. C. K. holding these large fish on very small hooks, I should think it very necessary that the hooks should be made extra stout in the wire, otherwise they would tear out.

Here is another prescription for catching mullet : Take the tough upper crust of a newly baked, plain bread bun and cut it in strips about half an inch wide. These should be kept in a tin for a few hours to toughen. Three-quarters of an inch cut from one of these strips is the bait ; the hooks used are small. The main line, which is used without a rod, consists of horsehair, at the end of which is a length of twisted gut ; the whole line is buoyed by means of small pieces of cork placed along it at intervals. If no fish are to be seen, breadcrumbs are scattered about, which may or may not bring them up to feed. When the whereabouts of the mullet are thus determined, the line is laid along the surface, the angler being in a boat, and more breadcrumbs are sprinkled around it with a lavish hand. The boat retires, the fish reappear, and if they have been educated up to buns, will surely be caught.

The object of having hair line is to obviate the rod. It is far easier to play a fish on a hair line, because of its elasticity, than on one made of hemp. A somewhat similar plan can be carried out by means of a rod and an ordinary undressed silk line well soaked in vaseline. This will float for a long time on the surface, particularly if a few small pieces of cork are used to increase its buoyancy.

I once saw a man fishing for and catching grey mullet from Dover Pier by means of a somewhat similar tackle. His line was of twisted silk ; just such a one as is used on the river Trent for chub, but perhaps a little thicker. At the end of it was a three-yard cast, such as we should use for lake trout ; at the end of the cast was a small hook, while at intervals of three feet were two droppers. The arrangement was, in fact, just like a fly cast made up for stream fishing, bare hooks being substituted for flies. But in addition, between the hooks, there were small fragments of cork which kept the arrangement from sinking. The end hook was baited with that slimy green weed which is found in harbours growing on the piles. The two droppers were covered with bread paste. The day was calm, which is the most favourable condition for mullet fishing, and the fish were now and again visible. The tackle was very carefully cast above the fish, and some breadcrumbs were sprinkled over the water. The line was worked very skilfully, and several fish of no great size were caught while I looked on.

In mullet fishing the element of individual skill comes very much to the fore. The tackle may be right and the bait may be right, but unless the angler can place the bait in a natural manner before the fish, he will have but poor sport. For instance, it is no use making clumsy casts and splashing down corks and baits on the top of the water, nor jerking the rod to get out line, thus making an inanimate piece of paste or macaroni jump about as if it were alive, in the most unnatural way. Except in the case of voracious fish, it is always desirable to make the bait look and act, if I may use the expression, as naturally as possible.

Mr. Senior in a later chapter describes the most artistic method of mullet fishing carried on at Nice by local anglers who wade in and, with a careful sweep of the rod, cast their lightly buoyed tackle beyond the waves. At San Sebastian somewhat similar gear is used, baited with small squares of salted tunny ; a favourite local ground bait consisting of chopped heads of sardines, potatoes, and clay squeezed up into balls. One of the Mediterranean pastes for mullet fishing is made from fresh roll mixed with pounded sardines or anchovies. As marine ichthyologists hold the opinion that the sardine is identical with our pilchard, this latter fish could, no doubt, be used in the same way. I have heard of officers stationed at Gibraltar, unable to catch fish by any other means, setting small trimmers for mullet and baiting them with paste, and ground baiting or surface baiting the sea all around with a mixture of breadcrumbs and water.

With regard to paste, that made from bread is better than the common flour paste. A piece as large as a pea will often suffice, unless, of course, there are fish of from six pounds upwards about. In the Channel Islands the chervin ground bait (see p. 123) is used. Few ground baits are more attractive than pilchard guts, and pounded green crab should never be forgotten. A large number of different hook baits have been recommended, including shrimps and prawns, both boiled and unboiled, but always peeled, pilchard guts, live ragworms, cabbage, silkweed, wasp grubs, fat pork, tripe, and gentles. An enormous mullet of about 12 lbs. or 13 lbs. was hooked by a bass fisher at Tenby, who was baiting with ray's liver ; the fish immediately ran out every inch of line, and then broke a strong, treble-plaited gut trace.

Generally speaking, mullet are caught more easily in salt water than in the brackish water of estuaries, and the best of all times to begin fishing is an hour before daybreak, if the tide suits. Of course, in places where the tide runs strongly we have to fish according to circumstances ; but wherever mullet are found unapproachable in the daytime, very early morning fishing should be tried.

The little there is to be written concerning fly fishing for mullet will be found on page 158.

To any who would condemn sea fishing on account of the ease with which the quarry are captured, may I respectfully suggest a short course of mullet or big bass fishing ?

The POLLACK, of all the members of the *Gadidæ* or Cod family, is, from a sportsman's point of view, by far the most important. When first caught it is a very beautiful fish ; its back of dark green bronze, lightening towards the sides, where it is marked with gold, the belly being nearly white. Soon after death, however, its back darkens, its lower portions become a dirty white, and the beautiful brown eyes get quickly glazed over. In shape it closely resembles the coalfish, but anyone who has once seen the two side by side will never mistake them, the coalfish having a bluish-black back and none of the golden brown colour of the pollack. Moreover, the coalfish has depending from its lower jaw a rudimentary barbule, while the pollack has none. As there are instances on record of fish having been caught which appeared to be hybrids between *Gadus pollachius* and *Gadus carbonarius* (coalfish), it is quite possible that the angler may at times be puzzled to determine the exact species of his capture.

The size of the pollack seems to depend very much upon locality. On many parts of our South coast one of 4 lbs. would be regarded as large, while at other places a five-pounder would be deemed a fish of no importance. Those I have caught on the north-west coast of Scotland ran from 4 lbs. to 11 lbs. in weight. Couch stated that he had a specimen weighing 24 lbs., and there is Lord St. Levan's Land's End fish of about the same weight. A friend tells me, however, that he has occasionally heard of fish weighing 30 lbs. to 35 lbs. : these are certainly very rare.

On the West coast of Scotland and off the Isle of Man pollack are, rightly or wrongly, supposed to follow the herrings, keeping at some distance seaward until the autumn, when their prey comes inshore and enters the sea lochs. When the herrings depart, the pollack follow, and pass the winter in deep water—such is the belief of the fishermen. The only reason to doubt this is that we cannot see beneath the surface, and it may be that the fish only take a bait well when herrings, &c. are about. The probability is that the smaller and more active school pollack follow the herrings, mackerel, &c., while the larger fish always haunt their fastnesses off headlands and rocky places generally.

Pollack are believed to spawn between Christmas and the early spring, the exact period probably differing, as it does with most fish, according to the locality.

Mr. Mathias Dunn, of Mevagissey, has placed on record an interesting account of porpoises attacking both the young and full-grown pollack. Some Mevagissey fishermen saw a battle of the kind taking place, and on putting about and sailing up to the spot, found that over thirty large pollack in a more or less moribund condition were floating on the sea.

There are very few places on our coasts where pollack are altogether wanting, but in apparently suitable localities they are occasionally very scarce. Small and medium sized fish are found in great quantities on the Devonshire coast, growing larger as we reach Land's End. So far as I know the best sport of all with pollack is obtained on the coasts of Scotland and Ireland, where, the fish not being very saleable, they are not sought after by the professional fishermen, and are, in consequence, very plentiful.

I rather incline to the opinion that pollack fishing is very easily overdone, and fishing grounds—more particularly those skirting headlands and outlying islands—more or less depopulated, at any rate for a time. When fishing is carried on over large submerged reefs of rocks, and generally in fairly deep water, the fish may be both scattered and plentiful, and no appreciable harm will result from the angler's attacks. But if you take a number of small channels between islands—little pieces of water which are almost like rivers and ponds—in a week's fishing most of the largest pollack will be thinned out, and the place may feel the effect of the attack for a considerable period. The same may be said of a solitary headland, a resort for pollack along miles of otherwise barren coast. I have seen several instances of spoilt pollack grounds ; take, for example, the end of Filey Brigg. At one time this spot had a reputation for large pollack, but now very few are caught there, the constant whiffing to and fro across the end of the Brigg having, it seems, thinned out the fish.

I once spent a few days at Scourie, on the west coast of Sutherlandshire (people go there to visit the island of Handa), and did a good deal of whiffing for pollack. I fished there for a whole day, catching only one lythe, as these fish are termed in Scotland. In the evening our man confessed that there were 'no many lythe' thereabouts. There used to be plenty, but he thought most of them had been caught. If we—a friend and I—would go a couple of miles down the coast we should do much better. So we forthwith set sail, arrived at the spot in question, and left our boat in a sheltered bay for the night. We walked over there the next morning and had some very fine sport.

The wanderings of sea fish are so mysterious and uncertain that I may be utterly wrong in my surmises ; but, in any event, there is no particular object in slaughtering these fine sporting fish by hundredweights. When forty or fifty pounds of pollack have been brought into the boat the rest might very well be returned. Unfortunately, these fish do not keep well, and, therefore, if a great quantity are caught they are as likely as not to be wasted. In fact, they are only fairly good eating on the day of capture, but superior to coalfish. They are greatly improved by being crimped as soon as caught, and make by no means despicable kippers.

The pollack does not possess so many local names as the coalfish, but is fairly well supplied in that respect. On many parts of the English coast he is always termed the *whiting pollack*, and the great North-country and Scotch name for him is *lythe*. Other local names are *leeat, leet, laithe, skeet, greenling*, and *greenfish*.

The pollack is essentially a rock fish, loving a free run of water, and frequenting the shallows rather than the deeps. I have caught large lythe in only four or five feet of water, and in the evening known them leap up into the air after a bright spinning bait as it was being drawn into the boat which had just passed over them. In the daytime they very much resemble pike, lying hidden among seaweed, ready to pounce out upon any passing prawn or fish, but rarely troubling to come to midwater or to the surface. Thus it has often been said that pollack fishing in the daytime is a useless proceeding, the fact being that the anglers have been at fault in not sinking their baits to bring them within sight of the quarry. I am not speaking of small fish, but of the large lythe one finds in the north of Britain. Small fish of one to four pounds are often very plentiful in fairly deep water where the bottom is rocky, perhaps congregating together in some little basin among the rocks, or other favourite place. There ragworm or live shrimp fished near the bottom would probably be successful. When such a spot is discovered, the marks should be very carefully taken.

A friend whose veracity is beyond question tells me that once when leaning over the boat and looking down through the clear, smooth water, he saw a strange sight. A pollack of 6 lbs. rose from the bottom and seized and absorbed a rubber eel which was hanging motionless from the boat. The day was sunny, which makes the incident the more remarkable.

The various methods of pollack fishing have already been described in previous chapters. Amongst others there is drift lining with live sand-eels, whiffing with dead ones on natural or artificial spinning baits, and fly fishing or whiffing with large sea flies. There is no absolute rule in the matter of pollack baits, the fish having what I may term local appetites. But the two which stand first and foremost are sand-eels—alive for preference—and a very young sea or freshwater eel. Almost, if not quite, as good are any small fish of elongated shape, such as the gunnel, variously known as butterfish and swordick of Orkney and the nine eyes of Cornwall. For moderate-sized pollack there are few more deadly baits than the large ragworm, which, on that account, is termed on some parts of our coast the pollack worm. Of artificial baits there are few better than a red rubber eel, sole-skin baits, and the red phantom. Often more successful than the foregoing are the feather baits mentioned in Chapter IV. They are sometimes found more effective in the daytime than the rubber eels.

The best pollacking is enjoyed during the early autumn, but a quantity of small fish are caught during the summer. On the coast of Devonshire thousands of small pollack are taken on whiffing lines in the early spring. A large number of baits (see Belgian Grub, p. 127) are used, and often several small fish are hauled in at once. About pierheads and suchlike places there frequently lurk a few pollack, and those who would catch them must rise early, before the water has been disturbed by boats, steamers, and paternosters, and let a single hook baited with a live pollack worm hooked through the head —the line being weighted with a half-ounce pipe lead—down among the fish, which, if not feeding very bravely, will often be tempted, particularly if a slight sink and draw motion is given to the bait. A few pollack are caught from Deal Pier in this manner during the early spring and summer.

When pilchards or any other fish or marine creatures on

which pollack feed are very abundant, the artificial bait sometimes fails ; then the angler should study as far as possible to
fall in with the passing fancy of the fish. A six-inch strip of
pilchard-skin together with a smaller piece of mackerel-skin is
often used as a bait on the Cornish coast. Three inches of
gurnard-skin is a good whiffing bait. Where the fish run very
large, large baits must be used. I have known success attend
the use of indiarubber eels, made by an amateur out of a piece
of black rubber tubing, double as thick and double as long as
the baits ordinarily sold in the tackle shops. The hooks on
which these indiarubber eels are mounted are tinned, and very
apt to be rather blunt ; indeed, when fishing in the daytime
close to the bottom the hooks are likely to come in frequent
contact with the rocks and so get their points smashed. It is
very desirable, therefore, to carry either a watchmaker's file or
a roughish quick-biting hone for renewing the point. Sharp
hooks are of the first importance in sea fishing.

May I again remind the tiro that the pollack is a powerful
fish and requires very strong tackle, and that this is particularly
the case in water of moderate depth where the bottom is rocky
and weedy, for headlong will the fish go into his submarine
fastnesses unless firmly held. There must be no yielding to a
pollack in his first rush, except in some places where the bottom
is fairly free from seaweed or the depth of water is considerable.

The COALFISH, a fine sporting fish, is remarkable for the
extraordinary number of aliases under which he passes. Ichthyologists have given him various Latin names, but these
fade into insignificance before the remarkable titles by which
he is known on different parts of our coast. He is probably
called coalfish on account of the nearly black colour of his
back, which, however, in some places is a dark green. He is
the *saithe* of Scotland ; in Cornwall they call him the *rauning*,
or *ravenous pollack* ; while the commonest name for him on the
Yorkshire coast is *parr* in childhood, and *billet* in middle age.
Coalsey, coal whiting, and *black pollack* are also common names,

and those who have visited the north-west coast of Ireland, and are taken out *glissaun* fishing, will recognise in their captures the *billet* of Scarborough. The Irish fishermen, by the way, have a theory which is very likely founded on fact, that when a glissaun or coalfish is hooked and is drawn through the water, its comrades follow it, regarding it as the leader of the shoal. Two lines, and often more, are used, depending from long bamboo rods, the bait being a rough wool-bodied fly. When a fish is hooked it is not drawn in until a second glissaun has taken a fly. Then one line is hauled in, and the other, with the unfortunate fish struggling at the end, left out for the shoal to follow. The sport, while it lasts, is fast and furious, and there is no difficulty in keeping a fish out on one of the lines. Mackerel fishermen have much the same idea. When fishing in fresh water I have often seen several fish follow one I had hooked and was bringing to the surface. Chub, perch, and sometimes roach will do this. Once a chub, hooked some fifteen yards from my punt, was followed in every turn and movement by another of about the same size which swam close to its side, and did not leave it until the landing net was about to be used. There are similar instances on record in the case of trout and, I think, salmon, in which both fish have been netted.

The late Dr. Day collected a number of local names for coalfish, from which I complete my incomplete list. *Sillocks* (Scotland) ; *blue-backs* (Yorkshire) ; also *baddock, bil, billiard, black pollack, black jack, bleck, coalsey, coal whiting, colemie, colmey, cooth, cuddy, dargie, gilpin, glassock, glashan, glossan, glossin, green cod, green pollack, gull-fish, harbine, kuth, lob, lob-keeling, moulrush, piltock, podlie, podling, prinkle, rock-salmon, saithe, sethe, sey-pollack, skrae-fish, stenlock,* and *tibrie.* The fry are variously termed *soil, poodler, billets,* or *billiards,* up to one year ; also *cuddies, saithes, coalman, saidhean,* or *suyeen* (Moray Firth), *gerrocks* (Banff), and *herring-hake* (Aberdeen). In County Down the fry are *gilpins,* next size *blockan,* then *gray-lord,* and adults *glashan.* In some localities the young are *cudden*, *pickey*, and *glassin*. At Portrush the following names are given according to the age of the fish : *cadan* (pr. *cudden*), *ceithnach* (pr. *catenach*), *glasan* (pr. *glashin*), and, when full-grown, *gray-lord*.

The name *cuddy* is, so far as my experience goes, commonly applied to the young of both pollack and coalfish in Scotland, but is, perhaps, more strictly the property of the young of the saithe. These little fish give rare sport to the fly fisher on a warm August evening, as I have described on p. 153. They sometimes come very short to the fly which, if fish skin, may have its holding powers improved by the addition of a small triangle just beyond its tail.

Coalfish are found on all our coasts, but are, perhaps, most plentiful off Yorkshire, in the north of Scotland, and all round Ireland. They are sometimes taken in the Downs by the whiting and cod fishermen. The coasts they appear to favour are steep and rocky, and when they come close inshore in the evening on the top of the tide, chasing sand-eels or the herring fry, they give grand sport indeed to the man who can cast a straight line and can play a fish.

Though found close to the shore, they like not such shallow waters as are frequented by pollack, the largest fish being taken in several fathoms of water on the edge of a tide-way. It is, as a rule, when feeding on the fry of other fish that they come close to the surface. At other times they hunt in shoals along the bottom in search of food, and may be caught on any ordinary bottom-fishing tackle. I have made several good bags of them on the Yorkshire coast when paternostering for cod, using mussels as bait. Coalfish spawn in the spring, and by August attain the cuddy size of about four or five inches, when little bare-legged youngsters sit on projecting rocks and catch dozens of them.

I have a lively recollection of initiating some ladies into this small form of sea fishing, one stormy day in the Lews. An immense trap dyke runs for some distance into the land, exhibiting on the coast a sheer wall of rock between two and three hundred feet high, which trends in gigantic steps down to the water. On one of these steps, in shelter of the rocks rising abruptly behind us, we sat in mackintoshes and cared little for a south-west gale which sprang up.

We began about low water, and then the little fish would only feed near the bottom. Our hooks were of the smallest, baited with fragments of the dwarfed mussels growing almost at hand among the crevices. As the tide rose, the fish came gradually nearer the surface, until, at the full flood, they were feeding within a foot of our little cork floats. The rain ceased, but the wind blew harder than ever, and I shall never forget our walk back to the lodge along the top of the cliffs. The whole country was running water, and every few yards small streams were pouring over the edge of the cliffs. But these hastily improvised waterfalls had not dropped a fathom before the wind caught them and hurled them back on to the moor, deluging us with the drainings of the land. However, home we brought our cuddies dead—eleven dozen of them—and delicate eating they proved that night at dinner. The following day they were soft and watery.

A friend living in the islands still further north caught no fewer than two hundred score of cuddies in one winter; but these were fish varying from three-quarters of a pound to one and a half pound. In Orkney there is a spring run of coalfish which go from ten to twenty pounds in weight, large numbers of which are caught by the fishermen, who trail small eels. Both in the Orkneys and Shetlands the liver is cut out for oil, the rest of the fish being often thrown away or used for manure. I believe there is an oily extract from the liver which is of service in tanning.

As food the coalfish is certainly inferior to the pollack, having a peculiar flavour of its own which is not altogether pleasant, and lies, I imagine, in the skin. This can, however, be overcome by judicious manipulation in the culinary department. An excellent way of dealing with a large catch of these fish is to have them kippered. I made the experiment some years ago, and the result was a success in every way. In fact, there is hardly a fish in the sea which cannot be treated in this manner. A kippered codling is certainly much better eating than the same fish plain boiled. Kippered mackerel, too, is a most estimable creation of civilisation. But it is, alack ! a thing to be eaten with caution, not to say fear, for the mackerel being a bad-keeping fish, it frequently happens that the unscrupulous fishermen, if unable to dispose of their take at a fair profit, sometimes hurry their two-days-old fish into the smoke house and produce an article which, though tasting well enough, is apt to work ill on those who eat of it. An imperceptible but very dangerous decomposition originates in the mackerel not very long after it has been caught. Beware of those which are dull as to their gills on the fishmonger's slab, or weedy as to their brown flesh when on the table.

But to return to *gadus alias*, which is as appropriate a term for him as any of those conferred by Linnæus, Pennant, Couch, Yarrell, and the rest. As the coalfish feeds on the surface, in midwater, and on the bottom, there is hardly a method of fishing described in previous chapters which will not suffice to take him ; but the best sport of all is certainly to be obtained with the fly rod when he is feeding near the surface. He rises savagely at the fly, like a fresh-run sea trout as yet in ignorance of the wiles of the angler, and if there is a big shoal of them, should one by any accident miss, another will take his place before the fly is lifted from the water. These fish are grand swimmers and full of pluck, and play gamely from first to last.

The very strong tackle necessary for pollack is hardly required for coalfish, for they can be played in orthodox fashion ; but there must be abundance of line on the reel, as a provision against conflicts with large fish. Whiffing you may take them ; paternostering you may take them ; and they pick up a bait lying on the bottom. But a mussel, or piece of fish skin, or lugworm, will be infinitely more attractive if moved through the water. If there is a slight bobble of the sea and we are fishing from a boat, it is best not to let the lead rest on the bottom, but to wind it up a foot or two, which will cause the baits to dance up and down and keep time with the motion of the boat. When these fish are met with, the angler should make the most of his time, for the shoal may not stop under the boat or close to the rocks more than half an hour. While there they will be caught as fast as the line can be cast in, the fish played and unhooked, unless the angler is a bungler. On the whole, I am almost inclined to say that *gadus alias* ranks higher as a sporting fish even than the pollack, though the latter takes precedence in this chapter as being more frequently sought after, and better known to sea fishermen.

SALMON and SEA TROUT are such undoubted *sea* fishes, coming into fresh water for breeding purposes, and possibly—in the case of salmon in very large rivers early in the year—for protection from seals, porpoises, and other enemies, that it seems right they should have a place in this volume. In dealing with the subject of fly fishing in the sea I have already mentioned a few places at which they have been caught in salt water. As a general rule salmon are too scattered to afford much sport. Compared with other sea fish, they are certainly scarce, and, all things considered, this is not surprising. Where they of necessity collect and are wedged up together, as in Loch Roag, Island of Lewis, a very long and narrow inlet, the angler has his finest opportunity. But in the broad mouths of great rivers the fisherman may toil all day and perhaps not present his fly to a single fish.

In America and Canada enormous runs of salmon occur, the fish being swept up by means of revolving traps arranged something after the fashion of a watermill wheel, thence turned down a trough, knocked on the head, and ultimately canned. The fish are in such enormous numbers as to afford very fine sport at the mouths of these fruitful rivers, particularly in Vancouver, where quantities are caught on spoons and similar baits both by sportsmen and the Indians. There, I take it, the sport results mainly from the quantity of the fish and their concentration in one particular part of the sea. If it should ever happen that, thanks to wiser laws than at present exist, coupled with their proper enforcement, our rivers should be freed from pollution and restocked by means of fish culture, then, I imagine, there would be many more places in which the sea angler might have an opportunity of plying his art on the king of anadromous fishes.

I should, however, mention here that on many rocks there is a tradition that salmon will not rise in the tidal pools, refusing the fly until they have reached fresh water. Sea trout, on the other hand, rise freely in brackish water.

SEA TROUT appear to hang about the coastline all through the summer, lying close to the rocks in the shelter of overhanging weeds, and may be caught in two to four feet of water. They are, too, far more plentiful than salmon. If in considerable numbers, they are, perhaps, best fished for in many places from the shore, the fly, or worm, or spinning bait being cast just over the edge of the weeds. An excellent bait, too, for the purpose is that cut out of a piece of sole-skin (p. 126). If, on the other hand, the fish are scarce, and it is necessary to trail a long distance to make sure of the bait being presented to a sufficient number, then, of course, a boat must be used. Such fishing, trolling, trailing, or spinning, as you please to call it, is carried on extensively in the kyles of Durness and Tongue with natural sand-eels or other bright spinning baits, natural or artificial. Very large sea trout are caught in this way, the tackle being much the same as would be used in fresh water. The amount of lead should be varied according to the force of the current and depth of the water; but just enough to keep the line from kinking, a quarter of an ounce or a little more, is as a rule sufficient, as the sea trout generally feed close to the surface. If the water be thickened by storms or flood water from rivers, then more lead should be used and the bait fished near the bottom. The lightest possible anti-kinking lead is shown in the illustration on p. 238. Note that the lead wire is placed *above* the swivels.

Some years ago naturalists supposed that there were several species of trout. Now, owing to the observations of fish culturists, who by keeping fish in their ponds have reduced this branch of ichthyology to a more or less exact science, the better opinion seems to be that there is but one trout, which is subject to variations in its appearance according to local surroundings, food, sex, and age. If it be rightly assumed that the fish in Loch Leven were originally sea trout which subsequently became landlocked, there is apparently no difference between a sea trout and the common brown trout of our rivers. In Loch Leven these fish certainly have an appearance somewhat suggestive of sea trout ; but in other waters they so change their appearance as to become indistinguishable from common brown trout. Here, then, we have sea trout, if my first presumption be correct, changing into rather remarkable loch trout and, when bred in the fish culturists' ponds, developing into ordinary fario. Assuming we are correct so far, the very interesting question arises whether the sea trout is a river trout which has left fresh water to seek the more abundant food supplies of the ocean, or the river trout is a sea trout which has pushed into fresh water to spawn and has taken up its abode in rivers ? Brown trout, sea trout, and salmon are evidently closely allied.

In the Antipodes the statement has many times gone forth that salmon have at last been acclimatised and been caught. The fact so far seems to be that the Antipodean salmon are ordinary brown trout which have left the rivers, taken to marine habits, and put on the silvery coat of the salmon or sea trout. A number of New Zealand trout recently were sent to Mr. Bambridge, of Eton, in a frozen condition by Mr. A. H. Strong, of Ashburton, New Zealand, with the following communication :

I have taken them in the *salt water*, and landed them in the breakers. All the fish taken at the mouth of the river are as white as silver, and the spots come out and show only after death. Higher up the river the fish are freely spotted and darker. The flesh varies from white to cream colour ; but I have had trout from

Lake Heron very deeply spotted, and with the flesh deep orange—not pink like char and salmon. There is no doubt that the trout go to sea, as they are caught in nets outside, and miles from the river. The strangest thing about these trout is that, although several varieties have been put into the river, we never seem to take any other variety than those I sent. I have put over 15,000 *Salmo fontinalis* in the main rivers ; but no one has ever taken one out, though when put into a small stream by themselves, they do well and grow to three or four pounds weight. They are then splendid fish and very game.

In British waters we have trout acting in just the same way, though not growing to the same size, and there is not much doubt that the ordinary brown trout and sea trout sometimes breed together, producing fish which are neither one nor the other. In the chapter on Fly Fishing I have referred to the slob trout of the Shannon and other Irish rivers. These estuary trout have received the attention of naturalists for many years. Knox, in his ' Lone Glens of Scotland,' published in 1854, refers to some taken at the mouth of the Nith, and also recorded fish of the same variety in the Kyle of Bute, Loch Fyne, the Forth, and the Yorkshire Esk. Dr. Günther describes specimens coming from Galway. Dr. Day, in ' British and Irish Fishes,' mentions them as common at Waterford. At Portrush, in Ireland, they are known as dolachan. These fish very frequently retain their red spots, and their river markings can be traced through the silver sheen. I have caught a good many in a tributary of the Shannon. In Norway it is a common thing to catch brown trout in the fjords a considerable distance from the river's mouth.

MACKEREL.—The mere name recalls pleasant visions of rippling waters flecked with white, of sunny skies, and the healthy, salt, sea breeze whistling through the rigging ; of a pile of little silver billets, two or three still quivering in the throes of death, and of a weather-beaten man with genial face who gently encourages us to continue hauling in those two-pound leads, breaking backs none the less. There are three hundred mackerel lying on the floor of the lugger, which means that we

MACKERELLING—'RIPPLING WATERS FLECKED WITH WHITE'

have hauled in our lines three hundred or more times. No ! friend, we have come for pleasure, not for toil. If you would add to the catch, take the lines yourself while we recline in the stern sheets and smoke, and hold that tiller smoothed by hardened hands on many a voyage.

Everyone is acquainted with the appearance and taste of the mackerel, but few would be the wiser for the telling that of branchiostegals it has seven, that pseudobranchiæ are present, that the air bladder when present is simple, and that pyloric appendages are numerous. He is a fish of brilliant colours, marvellous activity, and when fresh caught is most beautiful. *Scomber scomber* is his most approved classic title, but naturalists have several names for him, some asserting that there are several species, others that, as with trout, there are simply certain differences of appearance of no fixed character, all the mackerels being in fact one and the same fish.

The only local names for mackerel which I have come across are the terms *joey* for the shoals of immature fish a few inches in length which appear in the Bristol Channel in September ; *shiners*, a name used off the West coast ; and *harvest mackerel*, large fish caught at end of summer. The great majority of mackerel in the Bristol Channel appear to be immature, but are not so small as the *joeys* which weigh half a pound or thereabouts. Round about the rocks will be found fish three or four times as large ; but these are coarse and poor eating, while the half-pounders are particularly delicate.

Some of the finest mackerel come from Ireland. There the nets sometimes secure from 15,000 to 30,000 fish per boat. On many parts of the East coast of England large numbers of mackerel are caught by means of nets. Lines are not much used, the fishermen declaring that the water is too thick for the fish to see the bait ; but whether this view be correct or not I have never had an opportunity of testing.

On all our coasts this useful fish is more or less abundant, and is widely distributed over the more temperate portions of the world. Some of the best are caught in the English

Channel ; some of the worst, from an edible point of view, in the Mediterranean. As a matter of fact, we know very little about the wanderings of the great shoals of mackerel, beyond the fact that in winter they stand far out to sea, and in summer come close inshore. For years they may apparently forsake one portion of the coast and then return to it again in undiminished numbers. Such changes are possibly in consequence of the natural food supply having diminished ; as soon as it has regained its former condition the fish return. One of the earliest places at which mackerel are found inshore is Plymouth, the local boats sometimes taking them in February or March. But for our purpose they are a summer fish, and admirably serve to while away the time at many a seaside resort, the resources of which, natural and artificial, are soon exhausted.

Among the many reasons for which we should regard the mackerel with especial favour is the fact that they are, in their small way, tending to increase the wealth of an impoverished country, Ireland to wit. I see from the Fishery Reports that in 1893, 467,560 barrels of mackerel, valued at 152,512*l*., were caught on the Irish coasts, principally west and south ; and over 51,000 barrels of Irish mackerel were cured and sent to America. Pickled mackerel is to the New Yorker what salted herring is to the German ; and by the late failure of the American mackerel fishery Ireland has been greatly benefited. I am glad to say that the development of the West coast fisheries continues, thanks in a great measure to the active endeavours of the Congested Districts Board. In 1893, 6,579 vessels and boats, manned by 24,001 men and 1,215 boys, took part in the fisheries, showing an increase of 208 vessels since the previous year ; 730 more men and 240 more boys having become engaged in this work. We even find eleven Irish boats from Wicklow attending the Scotch herring fishery, a piece of enterprise which it is to be hoped was well rewarded.

Talking of enterprise, when the American mackerel fisheries failed, a fishing schooner from Gloucester, Massachusetts, sailed right away to Norway in hopes of making a haul of those very large and handsome Norwegian mackerel which in America fetch a high price. Owing to bad weather, only fifty-nine barrels of fish were captured. The return voyage, a distance of 4,400 miles, was made in twenty-two days. American fishermen have even visited the coast of Africa in search of mackerel !

There are some very tall stories related by old writers about mackerel. According to Ælian, the fishermen of his time used to train them to act as decoys, just as a little dog is trained to lead wild ducks into the hoop nets of the wildfowler. These remarkable fish would head a shoal and lead it into the nets which were ready spread. More than this, the progeny of these decoy scombers inherited the same remarkable powers. Then there is another story of a Norwegian sailor who went bathing, when a shoal of hungry mackerel surrounded, and nibbled and worried until by gentle persistence they worked him some distance out to sea. Assistance came in the shape of men in a boat, but it was with some difficulty the poor fellow was lifted on board, and he was in such a state of exhaustion from loss of blood that he soon died !

Another charming story, of the nature of so many found in popular natural histories, was once told by Lacépède, who quoted Admiral Pleville-Lepley as his authority. On the coast of Greenland are certain shallow bays which are almost land-locked. The water is clear, and the bottom of mud. There, throughout the winter, thousands of mackerel might be seen with their heads stuck in the mud and their tails pointing skywards ! As might be supposed, when they first resumed the vertical position at the advent of summer, their eyesight was affected, and they were netted without difficulty ; later on they were caught with hooks and lines. I love these old stories which writer after writer repeats so carefully, each with some little touches and additions of his own, just to give 'an air of verisimilitude to a bald and otherwise unattractive narrative.'

There are four methods of mackerel fishing. The largest catches are usually made by means of drift nets which are simply walls of netting, buoyed on one side, that drift with the tide during the night. The mackerel run against them, push their heads through the mesh, and are held captured. As the fish swim near the surface, the nets are not so deep as those used for herrings, and are often very much longer, eleven or twelve nets knotted together extending, perhaps, two and a half miles.

After mackerel have spawned in the spring they quickly recover their condition and, coming nearer the shore, take a bait eagerly. Then the net fishermen, in addition to capturing them in drift nets, use the seine, and surround the shoals which are seen breaking the surface inshore, chasing the britt or sile, as the young herrings and sprats are variously termed. At night I have known them to come on the sand in only a few inches of water, probably to feed on sand-eels. I have described at an earlier page how, wading on shore one night when my boat was stranded, I walked through a shoal of mackerel which made the sea beautiful by stirring up the phosphorescence. This phosphorescence, by the way, is sometimes called by the fishermen 'marfire' (i.e. sea-fire, from *mare* or *mer*), 'brimming,' and 'waterburn.' It is not favourable to drift-line fishing, as it no doubt discloses the position of the nets. On the other hand, it is helpful to the fishermen in search of the shoals, for as the fish swim near the surface their position is distinctly visible on the darkest night. I have heard of fishermen knocking a piece of wood against the outside planks of a boat, and when they noticed numbers of fish darting away, making a trail of light as they went, the nets would be shot.

Of line fishing there are three kinds : first, railing, whiffing, trailing, or plummeting, as it is variously called ; and much difference of opinion exists among fishermen as to the best gear to use for the purpose. I have illustrated and explained the different forms of tackle on pages 252 to 256. Though the ideas of fishermen vary considerably on the subject, there is little to choose between the various gear, except that some tow more steadily than others.

The bait of baits is undoubtedly the laske, or last, which is illustrated and explained on p. 97. Those who indulge much in mackerel fishing should provide themselves with dried gurnard or sole skin, to use as temporary laskes until a fish has been caught. A bait which is sometimes used with success when nothing better is forthcoming is a piece of tobacco pipe. Next the hook should always be two or three yards of gut, medium or stout according to the run of the fish, and the heavier and more clumsy the lead, the more distant from it should be the bait—in other words, the longer should be the snood. I need only add that for small mackerel the small hook shown on p. 238 should be used, while for larger fish the larger of the two will be better. These seem large hooks for so small fish, but the mackerel has a very big mouth, and the longer shank is a great advantage in enabling the fisherman to unhook the fish quickly.

The management of the boat is, of course, important. In the first place, it must be taken to the right fishing grounds ; and, secondly, it should be sailed at the right speed, which can be effected by carefully trimming the sails. The best time of the day for fishing is from daybreak till about twelve o'clock. If the wind is very light and the water clear, fish can be caught on very fine tackle when they will not look at the ordinary gear used by the fishermen. Under such circumstances the speed will be low and a very light lead should be used. Whether such heavy leads as are commonly used are really required I very much doubt. One summer, at Tenby, I fished persistently with a lead of about three ounces, while the fishermen kept to their two-pounders. I caught about twenty-five per cent. more fish than they did and with considerably less labour. It can hardly be doubted that the very large leads towed through the water tend to scare the fish.

The two remaining methods of fishing are from a boat at anchor. Off Scarborough and other places a fair number of mackerel are caught by means of an unleaded line terminated with a single gut snooding and a hook baited with the laske. The bait simply drifts out with the tide, and the bites of the fish are easily felt. The boat is usually moored on the edge of a big eddy just off the run of the tide. This is one of those methods which have been carried on successfully with the rod, and very pretty fishing it is when the mackerel are biting freely. I rather improved on this plan by adding a float and a half-ounce lead to the tackle and letting it out with the tide, and have caught a good many mackerel in this way. The float

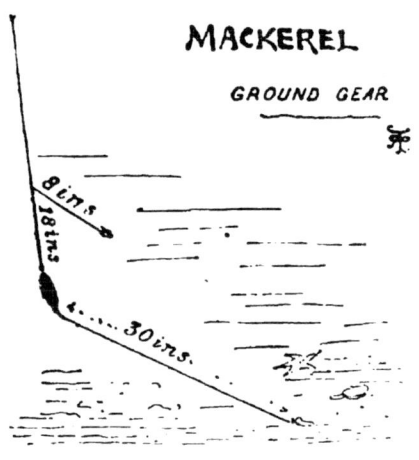

MACKEREL

GROUND GEAR

TACKLE FOR FISHING FOR MACKEREL
ON OR NEAR THE BOTTOM

enables one to see exactly where the bait is. To search the water thoroughly the pipe lead should be placed three feet from the hook, and the float, which is such a one as we should use in jack fishing (see p. 182), two feet above the pipe lead. For the running tackle there is nothing better than an undressed Nottingham silk pike line, such as I have recommended for fishing on the bottom.

About the end of summer mackerel begin to feed a good deal inshore, on the bottom, where they are caught on ordinary hand lines or with the paternoster tackle described on p. 218. A very good tackle for the purpose consists of the arrangement just described, minus the float, but the lead must be of sufficient weight to nearly hold the bottom. There may be two hooks, one at the end of the snood below the lead, the other attached to the line by means of an eight-inch piece of gut a foot above the lead. This fishing requires a good deal of skill, for the fish bite shyly and have to be struck at the slightest nibble. It is a great advantage to use a rod. Among good baits may be mentioned a very small sand-eel or half a large one, the hook being placed in at the mouth and the point brought out half an inch below the gills ; and mussels. On the Devonshire coast pilchard guts have been found an excellent bait, and a favourite plan is to cover the shank of the hook with a small piece of squid and put on the point of it either some pilchard guts or a small strip cut from the side of a pilchard. The lead should be lowered until bottom is felt, and raised about two yards. The professional gear for this method of fishing on the coast of Devon consists of a boat-shape lead with wire through it, and six feet of fine snooding. A favourite bait consists of a strip of very fine pilchard-skin, one and a half inch long by a quarter-inch wide, and an almost equally thin strip of squid about the same size. The two are just caught on the hook and are worked up and down, to give them an appearance of life, just above the bottom. This fishing ends about the beginning of October.

Off the Channel Islands ground fishing for mackerel is carried on a good deal at night. I have not used ground bait for these fish, but have not the slightest doubt it would conduce to a good catch. In America the mackerel fishermen have mills in which they grind up herrings for the purpose. Having attracted a large number of mackerel, they lower a bright metal fish which is well armed with hooks and then jig it about ; the mackerel rush to it and are foul-hooked.

When sport is not obtained either by whiffing or fishing near the bottom, various depths should be tried, for mackerel exhibit great susceptibility to changes of temperature, both as to their migrations and the depths at which they feed.

This concludes nearly all I think need be said about this admirable fish. When the mackerel are biting very shyly and the hook is being constantly robbed, I would suggest—and it is a mere suggestion, for I have not tried it—using Stewart tackle made up with large hooks, the bait being a strip of pilchard and a strip of squid cut worm-shape caught on and twisted round them. There is a two-hook tackle of this kind on p. 106. Three hooks might be better for this purpose. I have used this tackle for several kinds of bottom-feeding freshwater fish, other than trout and salmon, and found it answer extremely well, except in the case of tench, which mumble the bait and soon discover any hooks which are not well covered. Fly fishing for mackerel is referred to on p. 136.

Sometimes the plummeter will capture a fish in which the usual mackerel markings are replaced by spots such as are found on the back of a loch trout. This is merely a variety, *Scomber punctatus*, or spotted mackerel. There is also *Scomber colias*, the coly or Spanish mackerel, the latter name being the least desirable, as it is also applied to the tunny, and confusion engendered. This fish is not common in British waters. It may be instantly known by the eye, which is twice or three times the size of a common mackerel's.

The HORSE MACKEREL or SCAD is, according to naturalists, not a mackerel at all, but a member of the *Carangidæ* family, and has none of the usual markings on its back. A glance at its back fins will suffice to distinguish it from the common mackerel. In *Scomber scomber* the two dorsal fins are set wide apart, but in the scad they almost meet, and close to its anal fin are two spinous defensive weapons which the angler should avoid with care. A striking peculiarity of this fish is a lateral line, which crosses a number of scale plates so formed that they give the fish the appearance of having an external backbone on each side. These fish, which are common off Cornwall and are found all round our coasts, are fished for in just the same way as the mackerel, and take all the usual mackerel baits. They feed best at and after dusk.

The GARFISH, often found swimming with the mackerel shoals, is one of the most curious fish of the sea. It is long, eel-shaped, with a beak almost like a snipe ; the lower jaw, if jaw it can be called, projecting ; the back a beautiful bluish green, and the sides glistening with silver. This savage little fish, *Belone vulgaris*, is classed by naturalists in the same family (*Scombresocidæ*) as the flying fish. Of names it has enough and to spare : *long-nose, gorebill, sea-needle, mackerel-guide, needle-fish, gar-pife, horn-fish, guard-fish, green-back,* and *green-bone.* In Scotland they call it the *sword-fish,* the *green-ben,* and *green-bane.* On the east coast of Ireland it is called the *horn-eel, mackerel scout,* and *spearling.*

Garfish favour cold and temperate rather than tropical waters, and are found all round the British and Irish coasts, being particularly abundant off Kent, Essex, and Cornwall. They are a fish of moderate size, occasionally but very rarely reaching a length of three feet. In some places they swim in shoals, but in others are found singly. A few are nearly always mixed up with the mackerel, whose advent they are supposed to herald. Through the cold weather they live in deep water, appearing on our coasts in spring.

There are many curious instances on record of these fish having so savagely darted at their prey as to transfix them on their long snout. Several mackerel have been picked up pierced by the upper jaw of a garfish, which in some cases had broken off. In the 'Zoologist' is an account of a salmon peal (by which, I take it, is meant the sea trout of Devonshire) having been attacked by garfish. The long snout had passed completely through the thickest portion of the trout, which weighed nearly four pounds.

But sometimes the garfish itself is hunted. Mr. Dunn, of Mevagissey, tells a story of seeing one chased by a porpoise. For a hundred yards the fish and its pursuer rushed through the sea, the former continually throwing itself out of the water. When the garfish was almost overtaken, a projecting rock was providentially arrived at over which it leaped. The porpoise, on the other hand, ran its head against the stone, was more or less stunned, and gave up the pursuit. Garfish are great leapers, often springing high into the air ; and I have heard of their being caught by means of a net floated on the surface of the water. In the autumn large quantities are taken in the mackered seines. As a rule these peculiar creatures are not specially fished for by sportsmen, but numbers are caught when whiffing for mackerel, and angling with drift lines for pollack, bass, &c. They sometimes give off a very peculiar smell when first brought into the boat, and their flesh does not the more commend itself to the epicure by reason of the peculiar green bones. I have heard people say they were better than mackerel, but that is a matter of opinion. Certainly they make very good baits cut up into strips.

The SKIPPER, or SAURY, closely resembles the garfish. It is also known as *saury-pike, skip-jack, halion,* and *skopster.* The Scotch call it the *Egyptian herring, gosnick,* and *gowdnock.* It rarely or never exceeds eighteen inches in length, and may be distinguished from the garfish by five or six finlets which will be found between the dorsal fin and tail ; there are similar finlets near the tail, on the belly. The edges of its jaws are not serrated as are those of the garfish.

Very large shoals of skippers visit the coast of Cornwall at the beginning of summer, departing in the autumn ; and hundreds may sometimes be seen leaping out of the water at one time, this peculiarity no doubt giving them some of their local names. They probably do great harm to the pilchards, which they attack and sometimes transfix with their little sharp snouts. A few are sometimes caught on small baited hooks, but skippers would not be specially fished for.

The HERRING is a remarkable fish. I have often wondered why no one has written a book on him, for there is much more material for such a work than there is for a dissertation on any other of our food fishes. At the same time, I doubt if we really know more about the herring than we do of the salmon. There is a herring language peculiar to fishermen, fishcurers, and salesmen ; there are herring legends ; and there is a most powerful mass of fishery statistics. How many people, I wonder, know the meaning of *over-day-tart, matties* or *maties,* and *gut-pock herring*? *Sodger* and *soldier* we know, but what are these? *White-herring, green-herring, red-herring, black-*

herring, kings and queens—all these are terms of mystery ; possibly of deep meaning.   Let me say at once that an *over-day-tart* is a costermonger's phrase applied to herrings which have been kept over twenty-four hours without being salted, and have reddened considerably, owing to the extravasated blood near fins and gills.   A *gut-pock* herring is a Scotch term applied to fish which have made a hearty meal and distended themselves with small crabs, &c.   *Matties* or *maties*, a word possibly derived from maiden, signifies a herring which has not spawned and from which the roe is absent.   Fish full of roe, on the other hand, are in Scotland termed *mazy* herrings.

As for legends, there is no end to them.   According to a copy of the ' Banff Journal,' published some time in 1885, certain Buckie fishermen dressed up an unfortunate cooper in a flannel shirt with bars all about it, and wheeled him through the town on a barrel, like a cockney Guy Fawkes.   The herring fisheries had been very bad, and it was supposed that this proceeding would improve them.   There are even dark stories of men and women having been burnt for having cast their evil eye on the fishery and driven away the herrings.   It is, by the way, a common practice for whale fishers to burn an effigy to bring luck whenever a ship has fallen in with few whales.   The crew attribute their bad fortune to some unlucky person, and by burning his effigy they believe his malign influence will be overcome.   Needless to say, the unlucky individual is generally the must unpopular man on board.   If luck is exceedingly bad, ·two or three pictures or effigies are thus sacrificed.   It is possible that this ancient practice arose from just such a custom as that which prevailed among the herring fishers of Banffshire, by whom it may have been introduced on board the Peterhead whalers.

In Norfolk there was a curious theory that herrings and fleas made their appearance about the same time.   In ' Notes and Queries' a fisherman of Cromer was credited with the following remark : ' Lawk, sir, times is as you might look in my flannel shirt and scarce see a flea, and then there ain't but a very few herrings ; but times that'll be right alive with them, and there's certain to be a sight of fish.'

The Manx fishermen, who are particularly superstitious, think there is great virtue in taking a dead wren to sea. The idea appears to be based on an old tradition of some sea spirit which haunted the herring fisheries and brought storms. Assuming the form of a wren it would fly away, carrying with it, let us hope, all bad weather and misfortune.

Many curious theories have been put forward with respect to the migrations of herrings, but the generally accepted opinion now is that these fish simply retire to deeper water, returning to the coast at various seasons which differ with the locality. At the same time, they appear to forsake districts and parts of the coast for years together. The periods at which they spawn are very uncertain, and, like their movements, vary with the locality. From winter to late spring is the usual time, but it is quite possible that in some places they spawn twice during the year. From 10,000 to 30,000 eggs have been counted in a single herring. These when shed, unlike the eggs of most of our food fishes, sink to the bottom of the sea and attach themselves to the seaweed, rocks, and stones. In the Baltic herrings have been known to spawn in two or three feet of brackish water.

These fish feed variously at the surface, midwater, and on the bottom, many having been caught in trawl nets. From some very interesting observations made by the Scotch Meteorological Society it was proved that the weather had an important bearing on the movements of the herrings and the success of the fishermen. When there were thunderstorms about, the catches were small. Most fish were taken when the temperature of the sea was about $55.5°$.

I have included the herring within the scope of this book because of the undoubted sport they give to the fly fisher on occasions (see p. 160). The herring also takes bait, and at Peterhead, Wick, at the entrance to the Firth of Forth, and at Tarbert on the west coast, is caught on a dandy-line during the spring. The gear is nothing more nor less than a paternoster with little booms made of whalebone or stout wire about nine inches in length. The lead varies in weight from 1½ lb. to 4 lbs. There are half a dozen to a dozen booms, each of which is simply attached at its centre by a clove hitch in the line ; they are placed nine or ten inches apart. At the free end of each boom is about three inches of line terminated with a bright tinned hook. This arrangement is lowered to the bottom and then worked with a sink and draw motion. The brightness of the hooks attracts the fish. It is when the herrings are plentiful and are keeping near the bottom about or during the spawning season that this apparatus is used, those caught being usually cut up as bait for the cod lines. At night-time herrings will take a bait such as mussels, pieces of fish, &c., offered to them on any modification of the paternoster.

It is hardly meet I should say much concerning the economical side of herring fishing, but the figures are simply astounding. It has been said that during each autumn the nets in the North Sea, if joined together, would make a length of from 8,000 to 10,000 miles. On the Scotch coasts alone the annual take is over a million barrels of herrings, each barrel being worth over 1*l.* It is supposed that something like 2,000,000,000 are caught in British waters every year. Most fortunately herrings are prolific, for not only do we catch them in such enormous quantities, but all nature seems against them. There is hardly a fish in the sea larger than themselves which does not feed on them ; and, hunted from below, they are harried from above by wildfowl of every description, while porpoises, sharks, seals, all take toll from the shoals. From babyhood to old age the herring swims in constant danger of its life. If this slaughter by billions continues, it will not be surprising if Nature steps in and causes the herring to spawn three times a year instead of twice, to meet the demand.

In captivity herrings have been known to sacrifice themselves. They appear to be a gay, reckless fish, dashing hither and thither, believing that the sea is wide and obstacles few.

Some herrings imbued with this idea when placed in an aquarium, ran their heads against the glass and killed themselves immediately the gas was turned out. It was found that by leaving a small jet of gas during the night this self-martyrdom was prevented. Sometimes herrings revenge themselves in a wholesale way on the fishermen by simply crowding into the nets until their weight is so great that the warp has to be cut. Once, on the East coast, about 700 nets, worth 1,300*l.*, were thus sunk by fish.

The SMELT is a name given to three different fish. In the first place, the term is used locally instead of *smolt*—the young salmon, with which we now have nothing to do. There is also the atherine, or sand smelt, which naturalists do not call a smelt at all ; and lastly there is the true smelt, also called sparling (*Osmerus esperlanus*), which many people will be surprised to learn is a member of the salmon family. This, the true or cucumber smelt, has two back fins, that near the tail being *without rays* and fatty or adipose, like those borne by salmon, trout, and grayling. The atherine also has two back fins, but the one near the tail is of the ordinary kind with rays, while the back fin near the head is small, spines projecting from the edge of it like the dorsal fin of the perch. If the posterior dorsal fin of a doubtful specimen is carefully examined, there need be no difficulty in settling the question.

Everyone, I take it, knows the general appearance of these delicate silvery-looking little fish. The true smelt, when freshly caught, gives off a peculiar smell, which many people have compared with cucumber (possibly because it smells it is called the smelt). Some say that the perfume is of violets ; others, again, being reminded of rushes. For my own part, I say a smelt smells of smelt and of no other smell whatever. The Germans less politely have named it the *stinkfisch*. Taylor, writing in the ' Hardwicke Society Gossip,' asserted that he had known smelts come up rivers in such vast numbers that the peculiar cucumber smell was apparent to those who walked by the water's edge.

The true smelt is scarce on our southern shores, but very numerous from the mouth of the Thames northward. Many ancient and important smelt fisheries existed on that part of the coast. In the estuaries of the Thames and Medway these little fish are plentiful ; they are also caught in the Wash and Humber, and, in fact, in nearly all the tidal waters of that coast. Breydon Water, at the back of Yarmouth, is full of them in their season. They are fairly abundant in places on the West coast, and are caught in the estuaries of the Tee and Mersey, and all the rivers flowing into the Solway. Whether they are found on the Irish coast is uncertain.

Like salmon and sea trout, the true smelts push into fresh water for spawning purposes. They have been caught as high up the Thames as Teddington and Hammersmith. They spawn during the spring, and immediately after spawning are not particularly good to eat. Observers tell some curious stories of the way in which smelts on the East coast drive shoals of freshwater fish before them, as they ascend rivers. Roach and dace in large numbers are said to flee before the smelts in Norfolk waters. Something similar in relation to the dace has been noticed, or at any rate recorded, in respect of the Thames.

Smelts appear to grow very rapidly ; a contributor to ' Land and Water ' said that he had noticed in October ten or twelve which weighed together no more than a pound, while in March each fish would weigh four to six ounces, and a few as much as half a pound. Some of the fish caught were opened, and it was found that they had been feeding on herring fry. Their digestion must be rapid, for while those opened immediately on being caught contained the young herring, in those carried home was found nothing but digested food. Inside the herring fry taken from the smelts were small shrimps ! The gastric juice of the smelt would seem to be extremely acrid, for after making these investigations the observer wiped his hands on his handkerchief and then thoughtlessly used it to blow his nose, which caused his nostrils and lips to become inflamed, and his tongue to swell in an extraordinary manner.

Smelts are easily reared in fresh water. Colonel Meynell, of Yarm in Yorkshire, kept some for four years in a pond into which no sea water flowed. A similar experiment was tried with equal success in the lake at Roselherne Manor, Knutsford, Cheshire.

The ATHERINE, unlike the true smelt, is scarce on the East coast and abundant on our southern shores. It has a little family all to itself, named by Dr. Günther *Atherinidæ*. It is a widely distributed little fish, but is not common in Scotland ; and though, as I have said, rare on the East coast, is, I am assured by a careful observer, very abundant in Lowestoft Harbour. Great quantities are found in some of the Irish bays and harbours.

These little fish have some quaint local names. In the north of Ireland they are *Portaferry chickens*, *pincher* being another Irishism having the same meaning. *Sand smelt* is, perhaps, the most common name ; they are also called *silversides* and, in Cornwall, *quid*. The atherine does not, like the true smelt, push up far into fresh water, not going, as a rule, beyond the flow of the tides. It spawns during the summer close to the shore. Probably the greater portion of the shoals retire into deep water in the winter. With regard to fishing for smelts on the surface, in midwater, and at the bottom, I have written all that is necessary on the subject on pp. 161 and 188. It will be remembered that these little fish sometimes afford sport to the fly fisher, and are caught on the most delicate of tackle. Their excellence on the table also recommends them, but, as to this, the atherine is very inferior to the cucumber smelt.

Lightning Source UK Ltd.
Milton Keynes UK
UKOW03f1922060217
293762UK00001B/122/P